# WILD *about*
# FRESHWATER FISH

**Stoeger Publishing**
*Great Outdoor Books Since 1925*

**STOEGER PUBLISHING COMPANY**
**is a division of Benelli U.S.A.**

**Benelli U.S.A.**
*Vice President and General Manager:* Stephen Otway
*Director of Brand Marketing and Communications:*
  Stephen McKelvain

**Stoeger Publishing Company**
*President:* Jeffrey Reh
*Publisher:* Jay Langston
*Managing Editor:* Harris J. Andrews
*Design and Production Director:* Cynthia T. Richardson
*Director of Photography:* Alex Bowers
*Imaging Specialist:* William Graves
*Copy Editor:* Kate Baird
*Publishing Assistant:* Christine Lawton
*Proof Reading:* Celia Beatty

Published by Stoeger Publishing Company
17603 Indian Head Highway, Suite 200
Accokeek, Maryland 20607

BK0318
ISBN:0-88317-264-X
Library of Congress Control Number: 2002110165

Manufactured in the United States of America

Distributed to the book trade and
to the sporting goods trade by:
Stoeger Industries
17603 Indian Head HIghway, Suite 200
Accokeek, Maryland 20607

Third of six in the *Wild About* cookbooks series.

Printed in Canada

OTHER PUBLICATIONS:
**Shooter's Bible 2003 - 94th Edition**
  The World's Standard Firearms Reference Book
**Gun Trader's Guide - 25th Edition**
  Complete, Fully-illustrated Guide to Modern
  Firearms with Current Market Values

*Hunting & Shooting*
  Hounds of the World
  The Turkey Hunter's Tool Kit: Shooting Savvy
  Archer's Bible
  Hunting Whitetails East & West
  Hunting Club Management Guide
  Complete Book of Whitetail Hunting
  Hunting and Shooting with the Modern Bow
  The Ultimate in Rifle Accuracy
  Advanced Black Powder Hunting
  Labrador Retrievers
  Hunting America's Wild Turkey
  Taxidermy Guide
  Cowboy Action Shooting
  Great Shooters of the World

*Collecting Books*
  Sporting Collectibles
  The Working Folding Knife
  The Lore of Spices

*Firearms*
  Antique Guns
  P-38 Automatic Pistol
  The Walther Handgun Story
  Complete Guide to Compact Handguns
  Complete Guide to Service Handguns
  America's Great Gunmakers
  Firearms Disassembly with Exploded Views
  Rifle Guide
  Gunsmithing at Home
  The Book of the Twenty-Two
  Complete Guide to Modern Rifles
  Complete Guide to Classic Rifles
  Legendary Sporting Rifles
  FN Browning Armorer to the World
  Modern Beretta Firearms
  How to Buy & Sell Used Guns
  Heckler & Koch: Armorers of the Free World
  Spanish Handguns

*Reloading*
  The Handloader's Manual of Cartridge
  Conversions
  Modern Sporting Rifle Cartridges
  Complete Reloading Guide

*Fishing*
  Ultimate Bass Boats
  Bassing Bible
  The Flytier's Companion
  Deceiving Trout
  The Complete Book of Trout Fishing
  The Complete Book of Flyfishing
  Peter Dean's Guide to Fly-Tying
  The Flytier's Manual
  Flytier's Master Class
  Handbook of Fly Tying
  The Fly Fisherman's Entomological Pattern Book
  Fiberglass Rod Making
  To Rise a Trout

*Motorcycles & Trucks*
  The Legend of Harley-Davidson
  The Legend of the Indian
  Best of Harley-Davidson
  Classic Bikes
  Great Trucks
  4X4 Vehicles

*Cooking Game*
  Fish & Shellfish Care & Cookery
  Game Cookbook
  Dress 'Em Out
  Wild About Venison
  Wild About Game Birds

# Contents

# Introduction

This cookbook covers a dozen species of freshwater fish. In these pages you will discover delightful ways to prepare fish dishes, learn how to maximize tenderness and texture and find ways to increase flavor. Included are recipes to suit all tastes, from traditional fish dishes to the more exotic. You will find recipes for everything from daily meals to special occasions, all intended to please both the long-time fish lover as well as those who have yet to explore the culinary delights of fish. You will be delighted with the exquisite taste and texture of salmon, northern pike, trout, bass, perch and other freshwater species.

The best method for keeping fish fresh is to press them. This involves placing eviscerated fish on a clean cloth spread over a rack in a pan or container, then covering the fish with another cloth before topping it with crushed or cubed ice. With this technique, fish will remain fresh for five or six days of refrigeration. Just make sure they are kept covered with ice and that they do not soak up melted ice water in the bottom of the container.

In order to keep your catch longer, it must be frozen. Fish freeze well, but keeping them frozen for too long will alter and harden their flesh. Six months is recommended as the maximum freezer shelf life for fish. Also, follow these rules for freezing fish:

1. Always, wash, gut and scale fish before freezing it.
2. Wrap the fish properly in as air-tight a fashion as possible, using either a vacuum wrap or cellophane (do not use aluminum foil).
3. Always identify the fish when freezing it. Indicate the date it was frozen, and never refreeze a thawed, uncooked fish.

There are also some health-related precautions to be taken regarding the source of your catch. In polluted waters, fish can build up high levels of poisonous metals such as mercury. Consuming such fish can cause health problems, especially if they are consumed in large quantities. Avoid eating any fish from waters where authorities have posted warnings. It is also recommended that healthy individuals only eat their catch once a week. For young children, pregnant or nursing mothers, the elderly or those who are ill, this rate of consumption should be even less frequent.

***Note:*** *Each chapter discusses the best cooking methods for the particular species of fish it covers, but the fish varieties can usually be interchanged without drastically changing the recipe's final result.*

*Although it is not among the species covered in this book, the bones and trimmings from whitefish can be saved to make an excellent* fumet *(fish stock) that you can use to enhance the flavor of sauces and fish-based preparations.*

# Fish Stock

## Method

1. Melt the butter in a large saucepan and brown the fish bones for 5 minutes.
2. Add the vegetables and continue cooking for 5 minutes.
3. Deglaze with the wine. Bring to a boil and reduce the liquid by half.
4. Add the remaining ingredients and simmer for 25 minutes over low heat, without boiling.
5. Strain with a sieve and use as a basic stock for your fish recipes.

## Ingredients

| | | |
|---|---|---|
| 1 tbsp | butter **or** oil | 15 mL |
| 1 3/4 lb | whitefish bones and trimmings | 790 g |
| 1 | onion, chopped | 1 |
| 1 | leek white, sliced | 1 |
| 2 | celery branches, sliced | 2 |
| 2 | French shallots, chopped | 2 |
| 1 1/2 cups | sliced mushrooms | 375 mL |
| 1/2 cup | white wine | 125 mL |
| 1 | lemon, sliced | 1 |
| 4 cups | water | 1 litre |
| 1/4 tsp | thyme | 1 mL |
| 1 | bay leaf | 1 |
| 10 | peppercorns | 10 |
| 1 | bunch of parsley | 1 |

# Fish and Rice Soup

## Ingredients

| | | |
|---|---|---|
| 1 tbsp | oil | 15 mL |
| 1 or 2 | garlic cloves, chopped | 1 or 2 |
| 1 | onion, chopped | 1 |
| 1 cup | celery, sliced fine | 250 mL |
| 1 cup | fennel bulb, sliced | 250 mL |
| 1/2 cup | dry white wine | 125 mL |
| 5 1/2 cups | fish stock | 1375 mL |
| 2/3 cup | arborio **or** other round grain rice | 160 mL |
| | salt and fresh ground pepper, to taste | |
| 1 lb | fish, of your choice, in chunks (perch, walleye, bass, trout, salmon, etc.) | 450 g |
| 1/4 cup | fennel sprigs, chopped | 60 mL |

## Method

1. In a large saucepan, heat the oil and brown the garlic, onion, celery and fennel.
2. Moisten with the white wine and the stock and bring to a boil.
3. Add the rice and continue cooking until the rice is tender. Season with salt and pepper.
4. Add the fish and continue cooking for 3 to 5 minutes.
5. Check the seasoning and add the fennel sprigs just before serving.

# Provençale Fish Canapés

## I n g r e d i e n t s

| | | |
|---|---|---|
| 1 | red pepper | 1 |
| 1 | yellow pepper | 1 |
| 1 | baguette bread, sliced diagonally | 1 |
| 1 tsp | olive oil | 5 mL |
| 2 | garlic cloves, minced | 2 |
| 1 | French shallot, minced | 1 |
| 2 tbsp | capers | 30 mL |
| 1/4 cup | black olives, sliced | 60 mL |
| 1/2 lb | freshwater fish meat, cooked and flaked | 225 g |
| 2 tbsp | pesto (homemade **or** commercial) | 30 mL |
| 2 tbsp | lemon juice | 30 mL |
| | salt and fresh ground pepper to taste | |

## M e t h o d

1. Preheat the oven or grill to 400°F (200°C).
2. Cut the peppers in half, clean and grill them until their skin is blackened.
3. Remove the blackened skin and cut the peppers in fine strips.
4. To make the croûtons, place the bread slices in the center of the oven for 10 minutes or until they are browned.
5. Heat the oil in a skillet and sauté the garlic and shallot.
6. Add the peppers, capers and olives.
7. Incorporate the fish, pesto and lemon juice, and season to taste. Reheat and serve on the baguette slices.

# Fish Mousse Duo

## Ingredients

| | | |
|---|---|---|
| **1/3 lb** | whitefish, cooked | **150 g** |
| | (or pike, bass, walleye, crappie) | |
| **1/2 cup** | 35% whipping cream | **125 mL** |
| **2 tbsp** | fresh chives, chopped | **30 mL** |
| **2 tbsp** | lemon juice | **30 mL** |
| | salt and fresh ground pepper | |
| **1/3 lb** | salmon **or** trout meat, cooked | **150 g** |
| **1 1/2 tbsp** | lime juice | **22 mL** |

## Method

1. Chop up the whitefish in a food processor. Add half of the cream, half of the chives, and the lemon juice.

2. Process for a minute or two until the mixture thickens. Season generously with salt and pepper and set aside.

3. Using the same food processor (without rinsing), process the salmon or trout in the same manner. Follow the same procedure as for the whitefish, replacing the lemon juice with lime juice.

4. Fill small molds with the two mixtures, creating designs with the different colours of both mousses.

5. Refrigerate for 2 to 4 hours before serving. Serve with capers and red onion rounds. You can spread the mousse on crackers, or fill endive leaves with the mixture.

# Cumin-Flavored Fish Pâté

## Ingredients

| | | |
|---|---|---|
| 1 tbsp | butter | 15 mL |
| 1 | onion, chopped | 1 |
| 1/4 cup | white wine **or** fish stock | 60 mL |
| 2 tsp | ground cumin | 10 mL |
| 4 cups | potatoes, peeled, cubed | 1 litre |
| 8 to 12 cups | cold water | 2 to 3 litres |
| 1 tbsp | rock salt | 15 mL |
| 1 tbsp | butter | 15 mL |
| 1/2 cup | 10% cream | 125 mL |
| 1 lb | freshwater fish, cooked, bones and skin removed | 450 g |
| 2 tbsp | fresh chopped parsley | 30 mL |
| 1 | layer of shortcrust pastry | 1 |
| 1 | beaten egg | 1 |
| 1 | shortcrust pastry top | 1 |
| | salt and fresh ground pepper to taste | |

## Method

1. Preheat oven to 350°F (180°C).
2. Melt the butter in a large saucepan and sauté the onion.
3. Deglaze with the white wine, add the cumin and reduce until almost dry. Remove from the saucepan and set aside.
4. In the same saucepan, cook the potatoes in the water and salt. Bring to a boil and simmer until tender; drain and set aside.
5. Add the butter to the potatoes and mash until smooth, removing any lumps.
6. Add the cooked onion and season to taste.
7. Add the fish and parsley, and transfer to a baking pan lined with shortcrust pastry.
8. Brush the edges of the pastry with the beaten egg and cover with the second layer of pastry. Brush the top with the remaining beaten egg.
9. Cook in the center of the oven until the pastry is a golden brown, approximately 25 to 30 minutes.

# Trout and Salmon

## Trout

Trout belong to the salmon family. They live in coldwater lakes and rivers or, in some cases, in the sea, returning to fresh water to spawn. Trout fishing is an immensely popular type of sport angling, especially among fly fishermen. The body of the trout tends to be slender and laterally flat. There are three species prized as table fare—brown trout, rainbow trout and brook trout. The largest trouts can grow up to 55 inches (140 centimeters) and weigh up to 39 pounds (6.5 kilograms). The smallest species typically weigh a half-pound (250 grams) and measure 10 inches (25 centimeters).

The color of trout flesh varies, ranging from white to vivid pink, depending on the species and size of the fish. Generally, the delicate, much sought-after flesh of trout is semi-oily to oily. This is especially true for rainbows. It is important not to mask the subtle, savory taste of trout by camouflaging it with a complicated preparation. All of the recipes offered for salmon also lend themselves to trout cookery. In addition, trout is delicious when smoked.

## Salmon

Only one species of salmon inhabits the Atlantic Ocean, while there are five species found in the Pacific. One species lives permanently in fresh water. All other salmon are born in fresh water but migrate to the ocean, where they live for from one to four years before returning to their birthplace to spawn. Pacific salmon die after spawning, but this is not the case with Atlantic salmon.

Salmon varies much in size. The smaller mature species measure 24 inches (60 centimeters) and weigh 3.3 pounds (1.5 to 19 kilograms), while the largest can reach 40 inches (1 meter) and 40 pounds (18 kilograms).

Salmon is a fine, flavorful fish that lends itself to all cooking styles. As with trout, you do not want to hide its exquisite flavor through complicated preparations. Salmon is just as tasty served cold as it is hot. It can be kept for two or three days in the refrigerator, but care must be taken. Because of its high fat content, the flesh can quickly become rancid.

# Trout with Spicy Mango Coulis

**4 SERVINGS**

## Ingredients

| | | |
|---|---|---|
| 1 tbsp | oil **or** butter | 15 mL |
| 1 | garlic clove, minced | 1 |
| 1 | French shallot, chopped | 1 |
| 1/2 cup | white wine | 125 mL |
| 1 | large ripe mango, peeled and cubed | 1 |
| 3 tbsp | lime juice | 45 mL |
| 1/4 tsp | crushed chili pepper | 1 mL |
| 4 | trout fillets, 1/3 lb (150 g) each | 4 |
| 1 tbsp | oil | 15 mL |
| | salt and fresh ground pepper, to taste | |

## Method

1. Preheat oven to 350°F (180°C).
2. Melt the butter in a saucepan, and sauté the garlic and shallot.
3. Deglaze with the white wine. Reduce the liquid by a third.
4. Add the mango and cook covered for 7 to 8 minutes.
5. Meanwhile, place the trout fillets on a baking sheet brush with oil, and season with salt and pepper. Cook in the center of the oven for 12 to 15 minutes.
6. Add the lime juice and chili pepper to the mango mixture, and continue cooking for another 2 minutes, uncovered.
7. Remove the mango mixture from the heat and purée, using a food processor or an electric mixer, and season to taste.
8. Serve the trout fillets with the spicy mango coulis.

# Steamed Trout in a Citrus and Basil Sauce

**4 SERVINGS**

## Ingredients

| | | |
|---|---|---|
| 2 tsp | butter | 10 mL |
| 1 | French shallot, chopped | 1 |
| 1/3 cup | orange juice | 80 mL |
| 3 tbsp | lemon juice | 45 mL |
| 2 tbsp | lime juice | 30 mL |
| 1/2 cup | white wine | 125 mL |
| 1/4 cup | fresh basil, shredded | 60 mL |
| 5 | peppercorns | 5 |
| 4 | trout fillets, 1/3 lb (150 g) each | 4 |

## Method

1. In the lower pan of a double boiler, melt the butter and sauté the shallot.
2. Deglaze with the citrus juices and reduce for 1 minute.
3. Add the white wine, basil, peppercorns and citrus zests, and reduce by a third.
4. Cover the saucepan with the upper section of the double boiler, place the fish fillets inside, and cover. Steam for 5 to 7 minutes, depending on thickness. Serve immediately with the sauce and your favorite garnish.

# Italian-Style Trout

## Ingredients

| | | |
|---|---|---|
| 4 | whole trout, each weighing more than 1/2 lb (225 g) | 4 |
| 5 tbsp | olive oil | 75 mL |
| 4 | bay leaf | 4 |
| 4 | slices of pancetta | 4 |
| 2 | French shallots, chopped | 2 |
| 1 | fresh tomato, cubed | 1 |
| 24 | green olives, pitted | 24 |
| 2 tbsp | fresh parsley, chopped | 30 mL |
| 1/2 cup | dry white wine | 125 mL |
| | fresh ground pepper, to taste | |

## Method

1. Preheat oven or grill to 400°F (200°C).
2. Place each trout in the center of a sheet of greased aluminium foil.
3. On each trout, place 1 bay leaf and 1 slice of pancetta, and divide up the shallots, tomato cubes and olives over the trout. Sprinkle with parsley.
4. Moisten with the white wine and pepper to taste.
5. Fold over the aluminium paper to form packets.
6. Cook in the center of the oven or grill for 12 to 15 minutes, depending on the size of the trout. Serve immediately with seasonal vegetables.

# Poached Trout
# with Mushrooms and Mint

## Ingredients

| | | |
|---|---|---|
| 1 tbsp | oil | 15 mL |
| 1 | French shallot, chopped | 1 |
| 2 cups | sliced mushrooms | 500 mL |
| 1 cup | sliced oyster mushrooms | 250 mL |
| 1/2 cup | white wine | 125 mL |
| 1 tsp | fresh ginger, chopped | 5 mL |
| 1 cup | fish stock | 250 mL |
| 3 tbsp | fresh mint leaves, chopped | 45 mL |
| | salt and fresh ground pepper, to taste | |
| 1 1/3 lb | trout fillets | 600 g |

## Method

1. Preheat oven to 350°F (180°C).
2. In an ovenproof saucepan, heat the oil and sauté the shallot, mushrooms and oyster mushrooms for 4 to 5 minutes.
3. Deglaze with the white wine, add the ginger, and reduce by half.
4. Add the stock and the mint. Season to taste.
5. Place the trout fillets in the stock. Cover and cook in the center of the oven for 10 to 15 minutes, depending on the thickness of the fish.
6. Divide the mushroom garnish among four dinner plates and arrange the fish decoratively on top. Serve immediately.

# Trout in Lemon-Dill Sauce

## Ingredients

| | | |
|---|---|---|
| 2 | whole trout weighing more than 1 lb (450 g) each | 2 |
| | oil to baste | |
| Sauce | | |
| 1 tbsp | butter | 15 mL |
| 1/4 cup | green onions, chopped | 60 mL |
| 3/4 cup | white wine | 180 mL |
| 4 tbsp | lemon juice | 60 mL |
| 2 tbsp | lemon zest | 30 mL |
| 2 to 3 tbsp | fresh dill, chopped | 30 to 45 mL |
| 1 tbsp | fresh chives, chopped | 15 mL |
| 1 1/2 cups | 35% whipping cream (or 15% cream) | 375 mL |
| | salt and fresh ground pepper, to taste | |

## Method

1. Preheat oven to 400 °F (200 °C).

2. Place the fish on a baking sheet, brush with the oil and season to taste generously, both inside and out.

3. Cook the trout in the center of the oven for 15 to 20 minutes.

4. Meanwhile, prepare the sauce. In a saucepan, melt the butter over medium heat and sauté the green onions.

5. Deglaze with the white wine and lemon juice. Reduce by a third.

6. Add the lemon zest and herbs.

7. Incorporate the cream, bring to a boil and simmer until the sauce thickens, whisking to a smooth consistency. If necessary, thicken with a thickening agent (a tablespoon of flour mixed with a small amount of water).

8. Season to taste, and serve the trout with egg noodles and seasonal vegetables.

# Whole Trout with Honey-Flavoured Beurre Blanc

## Ingredients

| | | |
|---|---|---|
| 2 tbsp | oil | 30 mL |
| 2 | whole trout, weighing at least 1lb (450g) each | 2 |
| 1/3 cup | water | 80 mL |
| 1/3 cup | white wine vinegar **or** white balsamic vinegar | 80 mL |
| 1 cup | French shallots, chopped | 250 mL |
| 1 1/2 cups | cold butter, cut in squares | 375 mL |
| 1/2 cup | 35% whipping cream | 125 mL |
| 1/3 cup | warm honey | 80 mL |
| | salt and fresh ground pepper | |
| 2 tbsp | fresh tomato cubes | 30 mL |
| 2 tbsp | fresh Italian parsley, chopped | 30 mL |

## Method

1. Preheat the oven to 375 °F (190 °C).

2. Brush the trout with oil and season, place on a baking sheet and cook in the center of the oven for 15 to 20 minutes, depending on size.

3. To make the *beurre blanc*: in a saucepan over low heat, cook the shallots in the water and vinegar until they reach the consistency of marmelade.

4. Gradually add the butter, stirring constantly with a spoon or whisk until smooth in texture. Season to taste.

5. Add the cream and continue cooking for 1 to 2 minutes.

6. Add the honey to the *beurre blanc* and heat for 1 minute.

7. Remove the skin and bones from the trout before arranging on a serving plate.

8. Serve the trout with the honey–scented *beurre blanc*, and garnish with the tomato cubes and parsley.

# Salmon Chowder

## Ingredients

| | | |
|---|---|---|
| 2 tbsp | butter | 30 mL |
| 1 | leek white, sliced fine | 1 |
| 1 | garlic clove, minced | 1 |
| 1/2 cup | niblet corn | 125 mL |
| 2 cups | potatoes, cubed | 500 mL |
| 1 cup | peeled carrots, cubed | 250 mL |
| 5 cups | fish stock | 1.25 litre |
| 1 cup | white wine | 250 mL |
| 1 | bay leaf | 1 |
| 1 tsp | dried thyme | 5 mL |
| | salt and fresh ground pepper, to taste | |
| 1 lb | salmon, cubed | 450 g |
| 1/3 cup | 35% whipping cream | 80 mL |

## Method

1. Melt the butter in a large saucepan and brown the vegetables.

2. Moisten with the fish stock and the wine; bring to a boil.

3. Add the bay leaf and the thyme; simmer for 5 to 8 minutes over medium-low heat. Season to taste.

4. Add the salmon cubes to the soup and cook slowly for 2 to 3 minutes.

5. Add the cream, stirring gently, and check the seasoning. Serve immediately with crusty bread.

# Salmon with Fennel Sauce

**4 SERVINGS**

## Ingredients

| | | |
|---|---|---|
| 2 tbsp | butter | 30 mL |
| 2 | fennel bulbs, sliced fine | 2 |
| 1 | onion, sliced fine | 1 |
| 1/4 cup | white wine | 60 mL |
| 1 1/2 cups | 35% whipping cream | 375 mL |
| 1 | sprig of fresh thyme | 1 |
| | *or* | |
| 1 pinch | dried thyme | 1 pinch |
| 1 | bay leaf | 1 |
| | salt and fresh ground pepper, to taste | |
| 4 | salmon fillets *or* steaks, 1/3 lb (150 g) each | 4 |

## Method

1. Preheat oven to 400 °F (200 °C).
2. Melt the butter in a saucepan and sweat the fennel bulbs and the onion for 5 minutes over medium-low heat.
3. Deglaze with the white wine and reduce until almost dry.
4. Add the cream, thyme and the bay leaf. Cook over medium heat until the sauce thickens, and season to taste.
5. Meanwhile, place the salmon pieces on a non-stick baking sheet, season to taste, and cook in the center of the oven for 5 to 7 minutes or longer, depending on the thickness of the fish.
6. When done, place a large spoonful of the fennel sauce on each dinner plate, and arrange the salmon fillets on top.

### Note:

For a more exotic presentation, why not roll up strips of salmon and tie them with kitchen string before cooking in the oven. When done, always remember to remove the string before serving.

# Rum-Marinated Salmon

## Ingredients

| | | |
|---|---|---|
| **3 tbsp** | oil | **45 mL** |
| **3 tbsp** | amber rum | **45 mL** |
| **2 tsp** | fresh ginger, chopped | **10 mL** |
| **1** | garlic clove, chopped | **1** |
| **1** | lemon, sliced | **1** |
| **1/2 tsp** | crushed chili pepper | **2 mL** |
| **1 1/3 lb** | salmon fillets | **600 g** |
| | salt and fresh ground pepper, to taste | |

## Method

1. Mix the first six ingredients in a shallow dish. Season to taste.

2. Add the fish, cover and refrigerate for 30 minutes to 1 hour.

3. Remove the salmon from the marinade, reserving the marinade. Cook the salmon in a preheated oven at 400°F (200°C) or grill for 5 to 7 minutes.

4. Meanwhile, reduce the reserved marinade by a third in a small saucepan over medium-high heat.

5. Serve the fish over the sauce with your favorite seasonal vegetables.

# Grilled Salmon
# with Vanilla Sauce

## Ingredients

| | | |
|---|---|---|
| 1 tbsp | olive oil | 15 mL |
| 1 | shallot, chopped | 1 |
| 1/2 cup | white wine | 125 mL |
| 1/2 cup | fish stock | 125 mL |
| 1 cup | 35% whipping cream | 250 mL |
| 1 | vanilla bean, split and grated | 1 |
| | salt and fresh ground pepper, to taste | |
| 2 lbs | whole salmon | 900 g |
| 1 tsp | pink peppercorn | 5 mL |
| 1 tsp | fresh parsley, chopped | 5 mL |

## Method

1. Preheat grill to medium.

2. In a saucepan, sauté the shallot in the oil.

3. Deglaze with the wine, add the stock and reduce by half over low heat.

4. Add the cream and the vanilla bean. Reduce by half again or until the sauce takes on a smooth texture. Remove the vanilla bean and season to taste.

5. Meanwhile, cook the salmon on the grill for 5 to 7 minutes each side, depending on the thickness of the fish, until done in the center.

6. Just before serving, remove the salmon skin and bones, and serve the fish over a bed of the sauce. Sprinkle with the peppercorns and garnish with parsley.

# Salmon Steak
# with Tomato and Olive Sauce

## Ingredients

| | | |
|---|---|---|
| 1 | red onion, chopped | 1 |
| 3 tbsp | olive oil | 45 mL |
| 1 | large tomato, cubed | 1 |
| 3/4 cup | black olives, chopped | 180 mL |
| 1/4 cup | capers | 60 mL |
| 1 | juice of one lemon | 1 |
| | salt and fresh ground pepper, to taste | |
| 2 tbsp | butter | 30 mL |
| 4 | salmon steaks, 1/3 lb (150 g) | 4 |

## Method

1. In a saucepan, sauté the onion in the oil for 1 minute.

2. Add the remaining vegetables and the lemon juice. Season to taste. Set aside and keep warm.

3. Meanwhile, melt the butter in another saucepan and cook the salmon steaks until done, turning only once.

4. Serve the steaks accompanied with the sauce.

# Salmon Gravlax

## Ingredients

| | | |
|---|---|---|
| 1 lb | fresh salmon fillet, bones removed, with skin | 450 g |
| 1/4 cup | coarse salt | 60 mL |
| 1/4 cup | brown sugar | 60 mL |
| 2 tbsp | fresh crushed peppercorns | 30 mL |
| 1/2 cup | fresh dill, chopped | 125 mL |
| 1 | lemon, sliced | 1 |
| 1 tbsp | cognac **or** brandy | 15 mL |

## Method

1. Place the salmon fillet on a sheet of aluminium paper, skin side down.

2. In a small bowl, mix the salt, brown sugar, pepper and fresh dill. Cover the fish with this mixture.

3. Arrange the lemon slices on top, and sprinkle the cognac over everything. Fold in the aluminium foil to cover, and place in a shallow dish.

4. Refrigerate for 24 to 48 hours (24 hours for a soft texture, or longer for added flavor). The fillet should be turned every 12 hours or so, to prevent it from drying out.

5. Pat the salmon thoroughly, until it is dry.

6. To serve, slice the salmon in thin horizont strips or on an angle, beginning from the tail end.

7. Serve with toast, accompanied by a few drops of olive oil and fresh lemon juice, or a home-made lemony mayonnaise.

# *Black Bass*

**B**ass belong to the sunfish family. There are two major species, the largemouth and smallmouth bass. They inhabit lakes and rivers across North America and can reach lengths as long as 25 inches (65 centimeters). Smallmouth bass, sometimes called bronzebacks because of their coloration, prefer fresh, cool water and a rocky habitat. They measures 8-12 inches (20-30 centimeters) on average but can get much larger. Although rare catches over eight pounds are occur, any smallmouth weighing more than four pounds is trophy size.

Hardier than its smallmouth cousin, at least when it comes to acceptable habitat, the largemouth also grows larger. Its distinguishing characteristics include a black lateral stripe and a mouth that extends back to the middle of its eyes. Preferred largemouth waters include warmer ponds, lakes and slow-moving streams.

The word bass comes from an Algonquin word meaning "he who argues." Given the fact that bass are heralded for their fighting qualities, the description is an apt one. It is a sport fish that is rarely commercialized. With its lean, white, flaky and tasty flesh, bass lends itself to preparation in a multitude of ways. Most of the time, though, it is pan-fried, deep-fried or steamed.

# Pan-fried Black Bass
# with Tarragon Mayonnaise

## *Ingredients*

| 1 lb | bass fillet, cut in thin strips | 450 g |
|------|--------------------------------|-------|
| 1/2 cup | all-purpose flour | 125 mL |
| 2 | eggs, beaten | 2 |
| 2 tbsp | oil | 30 mL |
| 1 tbsp | butter | 15 mL |
| | salt and fresh ground pepper, to taste | |

Tarragon Mayonnaise

| 1 tbsp | Dijon mustard | 15 mL |
|--------|---------------|-------|
| 1 | egg yolk | 1 |
| 1/2 cup | vegetable oil | 125 mL |
| 1/2 | juice of 1/2 lemon | 1/2 |
| 2 tsp | fresh tarragon, chopped | 10 mL |
| | salt and fresh ground pepper, to taste | |

## *Method*

1. In a bowl, season and dredge the fish strips in flour.
2. Add the eggs. Mix well.
3. Heat the oil and melt the butter in a skillet. Deposit the fish strips in the skillet with a large spoon, and flatten gently. Brown on both sides until crisp.
4. Serve hot with the tarragon mayonnaise.

**Tarragon Mayonnaise**

1. In a bowl, mix the mustard and the egg yolk.
2. Slowly add the oil, whisking vigorously to emulsify the mixture.
3. Add the lemon juice and the tarragon. Season generously and refrigerate until serving.

# Black Bass Stuffed with Crab and Guacamole

**4 SERVINGS**

## Ingredients

| | | |
|---|---|---|
| 1 1/3 lb | black bass fillets | 600 g |
| | | |
| Stuffing | | |
| 3/4 cup | guacamole | 180 mL |
| 1 cup | crab meat | 250 mL |
| 1/3 cup | bread crumbs | 80 mL |
| | salt and fresh ground pepper, to taste | |
| | olive oil for basting | |

## Method

**1.** Preheat oven to 375 °F (190 °C).

**2.** With a sharp knife, cut out a pouch in the black bass fillet, without fully separating. Place on a lightly oiled baking sheet or in an ovenproof dish.

**3.** In a bowl, mix all the stuffing ingredients, and season to taste.

**4.** Fill the fish cavity with the stuffing, and fold the fillet over to close.

**5.** Brush the fish with the oil, and season with salt and pepper.

**6.** Cook in the oven for 12 to 15 minutes, or to your taste, ensuring that the stuffing is hot. Divide the portions and serve immediately.

**Note:**

Guacamole is made from ripe avocado that is crushed into a paste with lemon or lime juice and various seasonnings (usualy chili powder and red pepper). Sometimes finely-chopped onion, tomato and cilantro are included.

# Barbados-style Stuffed Bass

*This recipe is drawn from traditional Barbados cooking, where chefs stuff a fowl or fish before breading and cooking it in oil.*

## Method

1. Preheat oven to 400 °F (200 °C).
2. In a bowl, mix the shallots, lime juice, pepper, thyme and oregano, and the Worcestershire sauce together. Season to taste.
4. Brush the fillets with this marinade and place on a baking sheet or in an ovenproof dish.
5. Cook for 12 to 15 minutes, depending on the size of the fish. Serve immediately.

## Ingredients

| 4 | bass fillets, weighing at least 1/3 lb (150 g) each | 4 |
|---|---|---|

Stuffing

| 2 | French shallots, chopped fine | 2 |
|---|---|---|
| 3 tbsp | lime juice | 45 mL |
| 1 | hot pepper, chopped fine | 1 |
| 1 tbsp | fresh or dried thyme | 15 mL |
| 1 tbsp | fresh or dried oregano | 15 mL |
| 5 drops | Worcestershire sauce | 5 drops |
| | salt and fresh ground pepper, to taste | |

# Norwegian-style Black Bass Salad

## Ingredients

| | | |
|---|---|---:|
| 1 tbsp | chopped horseradish, in vinegar | 15 mL |
| 1 cup | sour cream | 250 mL |
| 1 | onion, chopped fine | 1 |
| 2 tbsp | fresh dill, chopped | 30 mL |
| 2 lbs | black bass meat, cooked and chilled | 900 g |
| 1/2 cup | 35% whipping cream, for whipping | 125 mL |
| 4 | hard-boiled eggs, quartered | 4 |
| 2 | tomatoes, cut in cubes | 2 |
| | salt and fresh ground pepper, to taste | |

## Method

1. In a bowl, mix the horseradish, sour cream, onion and dill. Season to taste and set aside.

2. Break up the fish meat and gently add it to the sour cream mixture. Cover and refrigerate for 1 to 2 hours.

3. Whip the cream and fold into the fish mixture with a spatula. Check the seasoning.

4. Arrange on four salad plates, and garnish with the egg quarters and the tomato cubes. Serve immediately.

# Parmesan-encrusted Bass

## Ingredients

Crust

| | | |
|---|---|---|
| 2 | garlic cloves, chopped | 2 |
| 1/2 cup | breadcrumbs | 125 mL |
| 2 tbsp | fresh parsley, chopped | 30 mL |
| 1/4 cup | olive oil | 60 mL |
| 1 tbsp | lemon zest, finely grated | 15 mL |
| 1/4 cup | lemon juice | 60 mL |
| | salt and fresh ground pepper, to taste | |
| 1/2 cup | fresh grated parmesan | 125 mL |
| 4 | salmon fillet portions, 1/3 lb (150 g) each | 4 |

## Method

1. Mix all of the crust ingredients together in a bowl.
2. Place the fish fillets on a baking sheet covered with parchment paper.
3. Coat the fillets with the parmesan mixture, patting the crust down on the fish.
4. Cook in a preheated oven at 400 °F (200 °C) for 7 to 8 minutes, or to desired doneness.
5. Serve with the lemon, accompanied with a starchy side dish and vegetables.

# Bass with Capers and Lemon Butter

## Ingredients

| | | |
|---|---|---|
| 1/3 cup | butter, room temperature | 80 mL |
| 4 tbsp | lemon juice | 60 mL |
| 1/4 cup | capers, chopped | 60 mL |
| 2 tbsp | fresh parsley, chopped | 30 mL |
| | salt and fresh ground pepper | |
| 2 cups | fish stock | 500 mL |
| 1 | whole garlic clove | 1 |
| 1/2 | onion, chopped fine | 1/2 |
| 1 | bay leaf | 1 |
| 1 pinch | thyme | 1 pinch |
| 1 1/3 lb | fish fillets, cut in 1/3 lb (150 g) pieces | 600 g |

## Method

**1.** Mix the butter with half of the lemon zest and juice. Add the capers and parsley, and season to taste. Set aside.

**2.** In a large sauce pan, bring the fish stock to a boil with the garlic, onion, bay leaf and thyme. Season generously.

**3.** Lower the heat and simmer the liquid. Place the fish in the hot stock and poach for 5 to 7 minutes.

**4.** Meanwhile, heat the lemon and caper butter slowly over low heat.

**5.** Remove the fish from the stock and transfer to serving plates. Coat with the hot butter and serve immediately..

**Note:**

Lemon butter can be prepared in advance; wrapped properly, it can be kept in the refrigerator for a week. It can also be cut into decorative shapes and placed on top of the hot fish fillets.

# Bass with Pistachio Sauce

## *M e t h o d*

**1.** In a skillet, heat the oil and melt the butter over medium-high heat.

**2.** Brown the fish fillets; remove and set aside, keeping warm.

**3.** In the same skillet, sauté the shallot and the pistachios over medium heat.

**4.** Deglaze with the white wine, and reduce by half.

**5.** Incorporate the cream and reduce until the sauce thickens to a creamy texture. Season to taste.

**6.** Serve the fish coated with the sauce, and accompanied with your favorite garnish.

## *I n g r e d i e n t s*

| | | |
|---|---|---|
| **2 tsp** | oil | 10 mL |
| **2 tsp** | butter | 10 mL |
| **4** | bass fillets, 1/3 lb (150 g) each | 4 |
| **2** | French shallots, chopped | 2 |
| **1/2 cup** | pistachio nuts,chopped fine | 125 mL |
| **1/2 cup** | white wine | 125 mL |
| **1/4 cup** | 35% whipping cream | 60 mL |
| | salt and fresh ground pepper | |

# *Perch*

Perch, though found almost everywhere around the globe, is rarely commercialized. The back of the perch is dark green or olive in color, while its sides are yellowish and delineated by 6 to 8 dark, vertical stripes. Its dorsal fins are brownish-green, with other fins being reddish or orange in color. The perch has a long, laterally flattened body, with the head accounting for one-third of its entire length. Perch measure from 10 to 20 inches (25 to 50 centimeters) and weight up to 7.7 pounds (3.5 kilograms). The average weight is much less, about 1.1 pounds (500 grams).

It is recommended that perch be skinned prior to cooking. When doing so, take care to avoid the sharp, spiny fins and numerous bones. Its flesh is lean, firm and white. Perch is often poached, pan-fried or braised. It can be prepared in the same manner as trout.

# Perch Curry

## Ingredients

| | | |
|---|---|---|
| 2 tbsp | butter | 30 mL |
| 1 1/3 lb | perch fillet | 600 g |
| 2 | onions, chopped | 2 |
| 2 | garlic cloves, chopped | 2 |
| 1 tbsp | fresh ginger, minced | 15 mL |
| 2 | tomatoes, peeled and cubed | 2 |
| 1 tsp | chili powder | 5 mL |
| 1 tbsp | ground turmeric | 15 mL |
| 1 tsp | ground cumin | 5 mL |
| | salt and fresh ground pepper, to taste | |
| 1 cup | plain yogurt | 250 mL |
| 1/2 cup | 35% whipping cream | 125 mL |
| 1 tbsp | fresh coriander, chopped | 15 mL |

## Method

1. Melt the butter in a saucepan and brown the fish; drain and set aside.

2. In the same saucepan, brown the onions with the garlic and ginger.

3. Add the tomato cubes, chili powder, turmeric and cumin. Cook over medium-low heat for 10 minutes. Season to taste.

4. Mix the yogurt and the cream; incorporate to the saucepan. Simmer for 5 minutes.

5. Gently add the fish to the curry sauce at the end of cooking. Stir carefully and serve this exotic delicacy with Basmati rice; garnish with the fresh coriander.

# Fillet of Perch with Banana Slices

## Ingredients

| | | |
|---|---|---|
| 4 | perch fillets | 4 |
| 1 | juice and zest of one lime | 1 |
| 1 tsp | oil | |
| 1 tsp | butter | 5 mL |
| 2 | ripe bananas, peeled and sliced diagonally | 2 |
| 1 | French shallot, chopped | 1 |
| 1/2 cup | white wine | 125 mL |
| | salt and fresh ground pepper, to taste | |

## Method

1. Preheat oven to 350°F (180°C).
2. Sprinkle the fillets with the lime juice and season to taste.
3. Heat the oil in an oven-proof skillet and melt the butter over medium-high heat.
4. Brown the fillets on both sides, turning only once, cooking for approximately 2 to 3 minutes per side. Remove and set aside.
5. In the same skillet, brown the banana slices and the shallot in the same oil. Add to the fillets.
6. Deglaze the skillet with the wine. Add the lime zest and reduce by half.
7. Return the fillets and the bananas to the skillet; continue cooking in the center of the oven for 4 to 5 minutes. Serve immediately.

# Poached Perch with Dried Tomatoes and Black Olives

## Ingredients

| | | |
|---|---|---|
| 2 cups | fish stock | 500 mL |
| 1 or 2 | garlic cloves, degermed | 1 or 2 |
| 1/2 cup | black olives, pitted and sliced | 125 mL |
| 1 | juice and zest of one lemon | 1 |
| 1/2 cup | dried tomatoes, cut in pieces | 125 mL |
| 1 tbsp | parsley *or* basil, chopped | 15 mL |
| | salt and fresh ground pepper, to taste | |
| 4 | perch portions, 1/3 lb (150 g) each | 4 |

## Method

1. In a large sauce pan, bring the stock to a boil.
2. Add the garlic, olives, lemon juice and zest, dried tomatoes and parsley, and season to taste. Simmer for 3 to 4 minutes.
3. Place the fish in the stock, cover and cook, simmering gently for 5 to 6 minutes.
4. Remove the fish from the stock, and use the tomatoes and olives as a garnish. Serve with your favorite pasta.

# Perch with Gribiche Sauce

## Ingredients

| | | |
|---|---|---|
| **1 tbsp** | oil | **15 mL** |
| **1 1/3 lb** | perch fillets, cut in pieces | **600 g** |

Gribiche Sauce

| | | |
|---|---|---|
| **2/3 cup** | home-made **or** commercial mayonnaise | **160 mL** |
| **1** | hard-boiled egg, chopped | **1** |
| **1 1/2 tbsp** | chopped capers | **22 mL** |
| **1 1/2 tbsp** | juice of 1/2 lemon | **22 mL** |
| **1/2 tbsp** | fresh tarragon, chopped | **7 mL** |
| | salt and fresh ground pepper, to taste | |
| **1** | garlic clove, minced fine | **1** |

Home-made mayonnaise

| | | |
|---|---|---|
| **1** | egg yolk | **1** |
| **1/2 tbsp** | Dijon mustard | **7 mL** |
| **125 to 2/3 cup** | vegetable oil | **1/2 to 160 mL** |
| **1 1/2 tbsp** | juice of 1/2 lemon | **22 mL** |
| | salt and fresh ground pepper, to taste | |

## Method

1. Heat the oil in a skillet over medium-high heat and cook the perch for 4 to 5 minutes each side.
2. Meanwhile, mix all of the gribiche sauce ingredients together, and verify the seasoning. Set aside at room temperature until the fish is done.
1. Serve the sauce with the fish. Your guests will enjoy this dish hot or cold.

**Home-made mayonnaise**

1. In a bowl, beat the egg yolk and mustard with a whisk.
2. Slowly add the oil, whisking constantly to emulsify.
3. Add the lemon juice, and season to taste.

**Note:**

Use home-made mayonnaise by itself or in recipes rather than using store-bought mayonnaise. Note: Home-made mayonnaise only keeps a few days in the refrigerator.

# Black Crappie Fillets Served on a Bed of Fruit

## Ingredients

| | | |
|---|---|---|
| 2 cups | sliced fruit | 500 mL |
| | (mango, pears, papaya, etc.) | |
| 1 | French shallot, chopped | 1 |
| 1 1/3 lb | black crappie fillets | 600 g |
| 1/2 cup | white wine | 125 mL |
| 1/2 cup | strong tea | 125 mL |
| 1 | juice and zest of one lemon | 1 |
| 1 tsp | fresh ginger, minced | 5 mL |
| 2 tbsp | olive oil | 30 mL |
| 2 drops | hot sauce | 2 drops |
| | salt and fresh ground pepper, to taste | |
| 1/4 cup | fresh mint, chopped | 60 mL |

## Method

1. Preheat oven to 350°F (180°C).
2. Place the fruit and shallot in an ovenproof dish.
3. Arrange the fish fillets on top of the fruit and moisten with the white wine. Cover.
4. Cook in the oven for 10 to 15 minutes, depending on the size of the fish fillets.
5. In a bowl, whip the tea, lemon juice and zest, ginger, oil and hot sauce with a whisk. Season to taste.
6. When the fish is done, serve over a bed of fruit, cover with ginger sauce, and garnish with fresh mint.

# Greek-style Crappie

## Method

1. Heat the oil in a skillet; brown the onion and the garlic for 2 to 3 minutes.

2. Add the tomatoes and herbs. Bring to a boil and simmer for 5 to 7 minutes.

3. Add the olives and season to taste.

4. Place the fish fillets on top of the sauce. Cover the skillet and cook over medium heat until the fish is done — 4 to 5 minutes, depending on the thickness of the fillets.

5. Serve immediately, garnished with Feta cheese and slices of onion. Accompany with a rice dish.

## Ingredients

| | | |
|---|---|---|
| 1 tbsp | oil | 15 mL |
| 1 | onion, sliced | 1 |
| 1 | garlic clove, minced | 1 |
| 1 can (19 oz) | crushed tomatoes | 1 can (540 mL) |
| 1 tbsp | fresh oregano, chopped | 15 mL |
| 1 tbsp | fresh chives, chopped | 15 mL |
| 1 tbsp | fresh thyme, chopped | 15 mL |
| 1/2 cup | sliced olives, choice | 125 mL |
| | salt and fresh ground pepper, to taste | |
| 1 1/3 lb | crappie fillets | 600 g |
| 1/2 cup | Feta cheese, flaked | 125 mL |
| 1 | red onion, sliced fine | 1 |

# Black Crappie
# with Honey-Mustard Marinade

## Method

1. Mix all the marinade ingredients.
2. Separate the fillets into four portions.
3. Marinate the fish for approximately 30 minutes, coating it with the mustard mixture. Remove the fish from the marinade without draining.
4. Heat the oil in a skillet over medium–high heat.
5. Meanwhile, dredge the fillets in the flour, and shake off the excess flour.
6. Cook the fillets in the hot oil for 3 to 4 minutes on each side. Serve immediately.

## Ingredients

Marinade

| | | |
|---|---|---|
| 1/2 cup | plain yogurt | 125 mL |
| 1/4 cup | whole-grain mustard | 60 mL |
| 3 tbsp | honey | 45 mL |
| | salt and fresh ground pepper, to taste | |

| | | |
|---|---|---|
| 1 1/3 lb | black crappie fillets | 600 g |
| 1/4 cup | flour | 60 mL |
| 3 tbsp | oil | 45 mL |

# Portuguese-Style Black Crappie

*Traditionally, Portuguese fish dishes use codfish and are accompanied with crusty bread and oven-baked potatoes sprinkled with coarse salt.*

## Method

1. Dredge the fish fillets in flour and shake off the excess flour.
2. In a skillet, heat the oil over medium-high heat, and cook the fish with the garlic. Season to taste.
3. Garnish the cooked fish with the tomato chunks, parsley and olives, and serve immediately.

## Ingredients

| | | |
|---|---|---|
| 3 to 4 tbsp | all-purpose flour | 45 to 60 mL |
| 1 1/3 lb | black crappie fillets | 600 g |
| 3 tbsp | oil | 45 mL |
| 4 | garlic cloves, degermed and chopped | 4 |
| 2 | tomatoes, cubed | 2 |
| 3 tbsp | fresh parsley, chopped | 45 mL |
| 1/2 cup | green olives, sliced | 125 mL |
| | salt and fresh ground pepper, to taste | |

# Sunfish Stuffed with Shrimp

## Ingredients

| | | |
|---|---|---|
| 4 | sunfish fillets, weighing at least 1/3 lb (150 g) each | 4 |
| 2 tbsp | butter | 30 mL |
| 1 | onion, chopped | 1 |
| 1/4 cup | white wine | 60 mL |
| 1 cup | small raw shrimp | 250 mL |
| 1/2 cup | parsley, chopped | 125 mL |
| 1 | tomato, cubed | 1 |
| 1/4 cup | milk | 60 mL |
| 1/4 cup | flour | 60 mL |
| 1 tbsp | oil | 15 mL |
| 1 | lemon quarter | 1 |

## Method

1. Cut a pocket in each fillet and set aside.
2. In a saucepan, melt the butter and brown the onion.
3. Add the wine and bring to a boil.
4. Add the shrimp and continue cooking for 1 minute, or until the shrimp are pink.
5. Add the parsley and the tomato. Season to taste.
6. Stuff the fillets and secure with toothpicks.
7. Dip in milk, dredge in flour and shake off excess flour.
8. In a saucepan, heat the oil on medium-high heat and fry the fish on both sides, turning only once. Sprinkle with the lemon juice and serve immediately.

# Sunfish with Zucchini au Gratin

## Ingredients

| | | |
|---|---|---|
| 1 tbsp | butter | 15 mL |
| 2 | zucchini, sliced | 2 |
| 1/2 cup | sliced mushrooms | 125 mL |
| 1 | garlic clove, minced | 1 |
| 3 | beaten eggs | 3 |
| 1 cup | milk **or** cream **or** half-and-half | 250 mL |
| 2 lbs | sunfish fillets, bones removed, cut in chunks | 900 g |
| 2 tbsp | fresh parsley, chopped | 30 mL |
| 1/2 cup | grated Swiss cheese | 125 mL |

## Method

1. Preheat oven to 350°F (180°C).
2. Melt the butter in a saucepan and brown the zucchini, mushrooms and garlic for 2 to 3 minutes. Remove from heat and set aside.
3. In a bowl, beat the eggs and gradually whisk in the milk.
4. Add the vegetables to this mixture. Mix with a spoon and season to taste.
5. Place the fish fillets in an ovenproof dish.
6. Pour the egg and zucchini mixture over the fish to cover, and sprinkle with parsley.
7. Cover with the grated cheese and cook in the center of the oven for 20 to 25 minutes, or until the cheese is golden.

# *Catfish*

There are several species of catfish, but those most often used on the table are channel catfish. Channel cats, which have comparatively sleek bodies with grayish-black backs and slate sides marked by scattered black spots, are a favored food fish. They are found in both rivers and lakes. A long-lived fish, channel cats typically reach lengths of 20 inches (50 centimeters) and weigh 3.3 to 4.4 pounds (1.5 to 2 kilograms); however, they can get appreciably larger.

Bullheads are a smaller member of the catfish clan found primarily in ponds and lakes. They have dark green or brownish skin, measure from 8 to 12 inches (20 to 30 centimeters) and weigh approximately .75 pound (350 grams).

Catfish have dark, fatty flesh, and that makes their meat best suited for being fried, poached or braised. Bullheads are often served sautéed in a seasoned flour coating.

# Spicy Catfish Cubes

## Ingredients

| | | |
|---|---|---|
| 1 lb | channel catfish, cut in cubes approximately 1 in x 1 in (2.5 cm x 2.5 cm) | 450 g |
| 1 | juice and zest of one lemon | 1 |
| 3 tbsp | oil | 45 mL |
| 1 | garlic clove, minced | 1 |
| 1 tsp | ground cayenne pepper | 5 mL |
| | salt and fresh ground pepper, to taste | |
| 1/2 cup | flour | 125 mL |
| 1 tsp | baking powder | 5 mL |
| 1 | egg | 1 |
| 2 tbsp | milk | 30 mL |
| | oil for frying | |

### Sour cream dip

| | | |
|---|---|---|
| 1/2 cup | sour cream | 125 mL |
| 1 pinch | ground cayenne pepper | 1 pinch |
| 2 tbsp | fresh parsley, chopped | 30 mL |

## Method

1. Mix the lemon juice, oil, garlic, and half of the cayenne pepper together, and season generously with the salt and pepper. Marinate the fish in this mixture for 30 minutes. Drain.

2. Meanwhile, mix the flour with the baking powder, cayenne pepper, lemon zest, and the salt and pepper. Set aside.

3. Beat the egg with the milk. Set aside.

4. Dredge the fish cubes in the flour mixture; dip in the beaten egg and dredge again in the flour mixture.

5. Fry in hot oil until the cubes are golden brown. Serve immediately with a sour cream dip.

**Sour cream dip**

1. Mix all the ingredients.

2. Set aside and chill until ready to serve.

# Poached Channel Catfish
# with Raspberry Coulis

## Ingredients

| | | |
|---|---|---|
| 1/2 cup | fish stock | 125 mL |
| 1/2 cup | white wine | 125 mL |
| 1 tbsp | raspberry vinegar | 15 mL |
| | salt and fresh ground pepper, to taste | |
| 2 tbsp | butter | 30 mL |
| 2 | French shallots, chopped | 2 |
| 1 cup | unsweetened raspberry coulis | 250 mL |
| 1 1/3 lb | channel catfish fillet | 600 g |
| 2 tbsp | fresh chives, chopped | 30 mL |

## Method

1. Bring the stock, white wine and raspberry vinegar to a boil in a deep skillet. Season to taste.

2. Meanwhile, in a saucepan, melt the butter and brown the French shallots. Add the raspberry coulis and season to taste.

3. Place the fish in the skillet with the stock and poach for 4 to 5 minutes, simmering lightly.

4. Remove 1/2 cups (125 mL) of the cooking juice, add to the raspberry coulis; stir in the chives.

5. Serve the fish over a dollop of the hot raspberry coulis.

**Note:**

You can find raspberry coulis at the market, but is easy to make at home by cooking raspberries with a few dashes of fresh lemon juice, salt and pepper. Simmer lightly for 5 minutes, purée and strain into a sterile container.

# Channel Catfish
# with Anise-Flavored Sauce

## Ingredients

| | | |
|---|---|---|
| 2 tbsp | butter | 30 mL |
| 1 | French shallot, chopped | 1 |
| 1 tsp | fennel seed | 5 mL |
| 1 | leek white, sliced fine | 1 |
| 1/2 cup | white wine | 125 mL |
| 4 grains | star anise | 4 grains |
| 1 tbsp | butter | 15 mL |
| 1 tbsp | flour | 15 mL |
| 1 cup | 35% whipping cream | 250 mL |
| | flour seasoned with salt and pepper | |
| 4 | channel catfish fillets, 1/3 lb (150 g) each | 4 |
| 2 tbsp | oil | 30 mL |
| 1 tbsp | butter | 15 mL |
| | salt and fresh ground pepper, to taste | |
| 1 tbsp | fresh tarragon, chopped | 15 mL |

## Method

1. In a saucepan, melt the butter and sauté the shallot, fennel seed and leek.
2. Deglaze with the wine and add the star anise. Reduce by half.
3. Meanwhile, mix the butter and flour to obtain a *beurre manié*★. Set aside.
4. Add the cream to the leek mixture and continue cooking for 5 minutes.
5. Meanwhile, dredge the fish fillets in the flour, shaking off the excess flour.
6. In a skillet, heat the oil and melt the butter over medium–high heat. Fry the fish for 4 to 5 minutes each side, turning only once.
7. Add the *beurre manié* to the sauce and continue cooking until the sauce thickens.
8. Season to taste and add the tarragon.
9. Serve the channel catfish immediately, coated with the sauce.

**★Beurre manié:**

a paste made of equal parts softened butter and flour that is used to thicken sauces.

# Catfish with
# Red Wine Sauce

## Ingredients

| | | |
|---|---|---|
| **3 tbsp** | butter | **45 mL** |
| 1 | onion, chopped fine | 1 |
| 2 | French shallots, chopped | 2 |
| **2 cups** | oyster mushrooms, sliced | **500 mL** |
| **3 tbsp** | flour | **45 mL** |
| **1 1/2 cups** | red wine | **375 mL** |
| **1/2 cup** | fish stock | **125 mL** |
| **3 tbsp** | 35% whipping cream | **45 mL** |
| 4 | catfish fillets, 1/3 lb (150 g) each | 4 |
| | salt and fresh ground pepper, to taste | |

## Method

1. Preheat oven to 400°F (200°C).
2. In a saucepan, melt the butter and sauté the vegetables.
3. Remove from heat and dust with flour.
4. Return to low heat, add the red wine, bring to a boil, and simmer for 5 minutes.
5. Add the fish stock and continue cooking for 5 minutes, or until smooth in texture.
6. Add the cream and season to taste.
7. While the sauce is cooking, place the fish fillets on a non-stick baking sheet. Season to taste and cook in the center of the oven for 5 to 7 minutes, depending on the thickness of the fillets. Season to taste and serve the fish glazed with the sauce.

# Catfish in Tomato Sauce

## Ingredients

| | | |
|---|---|---:|
| 4 | catfish fillets, 1/3 lb (150 g) each | 4 |
| 1/3 cup | all-purpose flour seasoned with salt and freshly ground pepper | 80 mL |
| 2 tbsp | oil | 30 mL |
| 3 | garlic cloves, coarsely chopped | 3 |
| 2 | onions, sliced fine | 2 |
| 1 can (19 oz) | tomatoes, cubed | 1 can (540 mL) |
| 1 cup | tomato juice | 250 mL |
| 2 tbsp | lime juice | 30 mL |
| 1 | jalapeño pepper, chopped fine | 1 |
| 2 tbsp | drained capers | 30 mL |
| 1 | bay leaf | 1 |
| | lime sections for garnish | |

## Method

1. Dredge the fish pieces in the flour and dust off the excess flour.

2. Heat the oil in a skillet, add the garlic, and brown for 2 to 3 minutes over low heat until the garlic turns golden. Remove the garlic and discard.

3. In the same skillet, place the fillets in the oil without crowding the bottom, and brown over high heat for 1 to 3 minutes each side. Remove from the pan, draining off any excess oil, and set aside on a plate.

4. Cook the onions in the same skillet until tender. Add the tomatoes, tomato juice, lime juice, pepper, capers and bay leaf. Bring to a boil, cover and simmer for 15 minutes over low heat.

5. Add any juices from the plate containing the fish fillets, increase the heat and continue cooking uncovered for 2 to 3 minutes to let the sauce thicken. Stir frequently to prevent sticking. Remove the bay leaf.

6. Arrange the fish on top of the sauce, cover and simmer over low heat for 4 to 5 minutes to finish cooking.

7. Serve the fillets immediately with the sauce, and garnish with the lime sections.

# Bass

### Striped Bass

Striped bass (or stripers) are a saltwater fish that move into fresh water to spawn, but fisheries biologists have developed ways to rear them in hatcheries and stock the species in fresh water. Their skin is olive green or bluish, ranging to dark black on the top of the back and being lighter on the sides. Silvery white on the underbelly, stripers have 7 or 8 dark horizontal stripes on their sides. The species can weigh up to 40 pounds (18.4 kilograms).

A lean fish than can be cooked in a variety of ways, striped bass do require a bit of special attention in cleaning. The readily visible "blood" line, which produces a strong and unpleasant "fishy" taste when left intact, needs to be trimmed away to leave only the white flesh. The fish is delicious grilled, braised, baked in the oven or used in soups or stews.

### White Bass

White bass live in fresh water all their lives, but migrate upstream to spawn each spring. With a dorsal color ranging from olive to grey and a silvery white underbelly, white bass can grow to lengths of 22 inches (56 centimeters), but their average length is 9 inches (24 centimeters). They have an average weight of 1 pound (450 grams) but sometimes grow as large as 5 pounds (2. 3 kilograms).

White bass are a fish with lean, soft flesh that has a delicate flavor. They can be prepared in various ways: pan-fried, braised, poached or baked in the oven.

# White Bass Fillets in Sesame Crust

## Ingredients

| | | |
|---|---|---|
| 4 | white bass fillets, 1/3 lb (150 g) each | 4 |
| | seasoned flour (salt and pepper added) | |
| 1 | beaten egg | 1 |
| 1/3 cup | sesame seeds | 80 mL |
| 1 tbsp | oil | 15 mL |
| 1 tbsp | butter | 15 mL |
| 1/2 | lemon, quartered | 1/2 |
| | salt and fresh ground pepper, to taste | |

## Method

**1.** Dredge the bass fillets in the flour, and dip in the beaten egg.

**2.** Cover with the sesame seeds and set aside.

**3.** In a saucepan, heat the oil and melt the butter over medium-high heat.

**4.** Brown the fillets on both sides, turning only once.

**5.** Sprinkle the fillets with the lemon juice.

**6.** Season to taste and serve immediately.

**Note:**

If you are making this dish using a fatty fish, it is not necessary to dredge with flour and dip in the egg batter before applying the sesame seed coating.

# Grilled Striped Bass with Tomato and Citrus Sauce

## Ingredients

| | | |
|---|---|---|
| 4 | striped bass fillets, 1/3 lb (150 g) each | 4 |
| 3 tbsp | olive oil | 45 mL |

**Tomato and Citrus Sauce**

| | | |
|---|---|---|
| 2 | fresh tomatoes | 2 |
| 1 | lime *or* lemon, peeled | 1 |
| 1/3 cup | white wine | 80 mL |
| 2/3 cup | orange juice | 160 mL |
| 2 tbsp | oil | 30 mL |
| 1 | French shallot, chopped | 1 |
| 1 tbsp | fresh herbs (either basil, oregano, rosemary or sage.) | 15 mL |
| | *or* | |
| 1 tsp | dried herbs | 5 mL |
| | salt and fresh ground pepper, to taste | |

## Method

1. Brush the fillets with oil and season to taste.
2. Cook on a preheated grill or in a serrated skillet for 4 to 5 minutes each side.
3. Meanwhile, crush the tomatoes with the peeled lime or lemon in a blender or food processor.
4. Add the wine, orange juice, oil, shallot, herbs, and the salt and pepper, blending well.
5. Serve the grilled fillet on a bed of lettuce, decorate with the tomato and citrus sauce, and accompany with your favorite vegetables.

# Striped Bass in Packets
# with Pineapple Salsa

4 SERVINGS

## Ingredients

### Salsa

| | | |
|---|---|---|
| 1 1/2 cups | fresh or canned pineapple, cubed | 375 mL |
| 1 | tomato, seeded and cubed | 1 |
| 1/4 cup | fresh coriander, chopped | 60 mL |
| 3 tbsp | red onion, chopped | 45 mL |
| 1/2 tbsp | sugar | 7 mL |

### Striped Bass Packets

| | | |
|---|---|---|
| 1 | small onion, cut in thin slices | 1 |
| 3 tbsp | soy sauce | 45 mL |
| 1/4 cup | oil | 60 mL |
| 3 tbsp | lime juice | 45 mL |
| 1 | garlic clove, minced | 1 |
| 4 | pieces of striped bass, weighing 1/3 lb (150 g) each | 4 |
| 4 | sprigs of fresh coriander | 4 |
| | salt and fresh ground pepper, to taste | |

## Method

1. Mix all the salsa ingredients in a bowl. Season with salt and pepper to taste and refrigerate or set aside in a cool place (may be made 2 hours in advance).

2. In a shallow dish (not aluminium), combine the sliced onion, soy sauce, oil, lime juice and the garlic.

3. Add the fish, turning to coat with the soy mixture. Cover and marinate for 30 minutes.

4. Prepare four squares of aluminium foil, and place a square of parchment paper on each. Place each piece of fish in the center of the paper, and divide the remaining marinade among the fish pieces, to taste.

5. Garnish with a sprig of coriander, fold the corners of each piece of aluminium foil to form a packet, and seal tight.

6. Cook the fish on a grill or in an oven preheated to 400°F (200°C) for 8 to 10 minutes. Serve the fish immediately with the salsa.

# Oriental-Style Striped Bass

**4 SERVINGS**

## Ingredients

| | | |
|---|---|---|
| 2 tbsp | oil | 30 mL |
| 5 | green onions, chopped | 5 |
| 1 or 2 | garlic cloves, chopped | 1 or 2 |
| 1 tbsp | fresh ginger, minced | 15 mL |
| 4 | shiitake mushrooms, sliced fine | 4 |
| 1 1/3 lb | striped bass fillet | 600 g |
| 1 tbsp | cornstarch | 15 mL |
| 2 to 3 tbsp | soy sauce | 30 to 45 mL |
| 1 1/2 tbsp | sesame seed oil | 22 mL |
| 1 cup | fish stock | 250 mL |
| 1 1/2 tbsp | fish sauce (Nuoc Nam)* | 22 mL |
| 1 pinch | Chinese five spice powder* | 1 pinch |
| 2 tbsp | sugar *or* honey | 30 mL |

## Method

**1.** Heat half the oil in a large skillet; sauté the green onions, garlic, ginger and mushrooms. Set aside.

**2.** In the same skillet, brown the fish in the remaining oil over high heat.

**3.** Meanwhile, mix the remaining ingredients with the vegetables and ginger. Pour over the fish and simmer over low heat to allow the sauce to thicken. If necessary, finish cooking the fish in the sauce before serving with rice noodles and crispy spinach as side dishes.

**\*Note:**

Nuoc Nam – available in Asian markets.

**\*Note:**

Chinese five-spice powder is available in Asian markets or you can make your own by blending equal amounts of cinnamon, cloves, fennel seed, star anise and Szechuan peppercorns.

# Striped Bass
# with Carrot-Peach Coulis

## Ingredients

Carrot-Peach Coulis

| | | |
|---|---|---|
| 1 | onion, chopped | 1 |
| | *or* | |
| 2 | French shallots, chopped | 2 |
| 3 | large carrots, cut in small cubes *or* finely sliced | 3 |
| 1 tbsp | butter *or* oil | 15 mL |
| 3 tbsp | white wine | 45 mL |
| 1/2 cup | fish stock | 125 mL |
| 1 | ripe peach, peeled and cubed | 1 |
| | | |
| 4 | striped bass steaks, 1/3 lb (150 g) each | 4 |
| | salt and fresh ground pepper, to taste | |

## Method

**Carrot-Peach Coulis**

1. Preheat grill to medium–high, or the oven to 400°F (200°C).

2. In a saucepan, sauté the onion and the carrots in butter over medium-high heat.

3. Deglaze with the white wine and reduce by half.

4. Add the stock and simmer over medium heat for 8 to 10 minutes.

5. Add the peach and continue cooking for 5 minutes.

6. Reduce to a purée in a food processor or with an electric mixer until smooth in texture, and season to taste. Set aside and keep warm.

7. Grill the steaks for 10 to 15 minutes, turning only once. Cooking time will vary depending on the thickness of the steaks.

8. Serve the striped bass covered with the coulis, and accompany with your favorite vegetables.

# Broiled Striped Bass with Avocado and Pink Grapefruit

## Ingredients

Vinaigrette

| | | |
|---|---|---|
| **1 cup** | pink grapefruit juice | **250 mL** |
| **3 tbsp** | maple syrup | **45 mL** |
| **1 tbsp** | Dijon-style mustard | **15 mL** |
| | salt and fresh ground pepper, to taste | |
| **2** | ripe avocados, sliced | **2** |
| **2** | pink grapefruit, in sections or sliced, skin removed | **2** |
| **1 tbsp** | Dijon mustard | **15 mL** |
| **4** | striped bass fillets or steaks, 1/3 lb (150 g) each | **4** |

## Method

1. Make the vinaigrette by thoroughly mixing all the ingredients. Whisk the mixture to obtain a smooth, creamy texture.

2. Place the fillets in a shallow dish and pour half of the vinaigrette over them. Marinate for 45 minutes to 1 hour in the refrigerator.

3. Remove the fish from the marinade and grill on the barbecue or in a serrated skillet preheated to medium–high heat.

4. Meanwhile, pour the remaining vinaigrette over the avocado and grapefruit slices, and divide onto serving dishes.

5. Decoratively arrange the grilled fish on top, and serve with rice.

# *Walleye*

Walleye are members of the perch family. They live in cool or cold freshwater lakes and large rivers in northern latitudes. Walleye are easily distinguished from pike—having two dorsal fins to the pike's single one. The walleye has a long, rather flat body, and a large mouth filled with tiny, razor-sharp teeth. Its back and sides are colored a brownish-olive green, sometimes even tending toward yellow. The top and flanks of walleye have golden spots and dark oblique lines, while the underbelly is white. The largest member of the perch family, walleye can reach a length of 12 to 22 inches (30 to 55 centimeters) and weigh up to 11 pounds.

Walleye is a firm-fleshed fish like perch and pike. It lends itself to preparation in the same manner as these two fish. One of the tastiest of all freshwater fish species, walleye can be cooked using a variety of techniques. They are often cooked whole or in fillets. The delicate flesh is lean and white.

# Walleye Paupiettes with Spinach and Cheese Filling

**4 SERVINGS**

## Ingredients

| | | |
|---|---|---|
| 4 | walleye fillets, 1/3 lb (150 g) each | 4 |
| 4 | slices of Swiss or other cheese | 4 |
| 1 package (1/2 lb) | fresh spinach, washed, stems removed | 1 package (225 g) |
| 1 | red pepper, cut in strips | 1 |
| 1 | French shallot, chopped | 1 |
| 2 tsp | butter | 10 mL |
| 3/4 cup | water *or* fish stock | 180 mL |
| | salt and fresh ground pepper, to taste | |

## Method

1. Place the fish fillets on a work surface and season with salt and pepper.

2. Lay the cheese slices on top of the fish fillets. Cover with the spinach leaves and add a strip of red pepper to the small end of the fillets. Set aside the remaining red pepper.

3. Roll the paupiettes, beginning from the small end, tying them with kitchen string or toothpicks. Place in a greased ovenproof dish.

4. Cook in the oven at 350°F (180°C) for 12 to 15 minutes or until done.

5. Meanwhile, sauté the shallot in a saucepan with butter, along with the remaining spinach.

6. Add the water and salt and pepper, and bring to a boil. Reduce the heat and simmer for 10 minutes.

7. Blend the mixture in a food processor or by hand to obtain a coulis, and check the seasoning.

8. Spoon out the coulis onto the bottom of a serving plate, add the paupiettes and decorate with the remaining diced or julienned red pepper.

9. Serve hot with a starchy side dish and hot vegetables, or with a salad.

# Walleye Cooked in Gingered Beer Sauce

## Ingredients

| | | |
|---|---|---|
| 2 tbsp | oil | 30 mL |
| 1 | onion, sliced | 1 |
| 2 | garlic cloves, chopped | 2 |
| 1 cup | yellow beans, halved | 250 mL |
| 2 | zucchini, sliced | 2 |
| 2 | carrots, sliced | 2 |
| 1 | red pepper, cut in strips | 1 |
| 1 tbsp | fresh ginger, minced | 15 mL |
| 1 bottle (12 oz) | pale ale | 1 bottle (341 mL) |
| | salt and fresh ground pepper, to taste | |
| 1 1/3 lb | walleye, cut in cubes | 600 g |

### Beurre Manié*

| | | |
|---|---|---|
| 1 tbsp | butter | 15 mL |
| 1 tbsp | flour | 15 mL |

## Method

1. Heat the oil in a skillet and sauté the vegetables and ginger for 3 to 4 minutes.
2. Add the beer, bring to a boil, and let simmer for 2 minutes. Season to taste with the salt and pepper.
3. Place the fish cubes in the beer and cook covered for 3 to 4 minutes.
4. Remove the fish and the vegetables.
5. Thicken the sauce with the butter and flour mix (*beurre manié*).
6. Return the fish and the vegetables to the sauce, reheat and serve over a bed of rice. Garnish with sprigs of fresh coriander.

**\*Beurre manié:**

a paste made of equal parts softened butter and flour that is used to thicken sauces.

# Walleye Ratatouille

## Ingredients

Ratatouille

| | | |
|---|---|---|
| **2 tbsp** | olive oil | 30 mL |
| 1 | zucchini, cubed | 1 |
| 1 | yellow zucchini, cubed | 1 |
| 1 | red pepper, cubed | 1 |
| 1 | green pepper, cubed | 1 |
| **1 1/2 cups** | mushrooms, quartered | 375 mL |
| 1 | onion, sliced | 1 |
| **2 or 3** | garlic cloves, sliced fine | **2 or 3** |
| **1 cup** | home-made *or* commercial tomato sauce | 250 mL |
| | salt and fresh ground pepper, to taste | |
| | basil and oregano, fresh *or* dried, to taste | |
| **1 1/2 cups** | fish stock | 375 mL |
| 1 | sprig of fresh oregano | 1 |
| | **or** | |
| **1 tsp** | dried oregano | 5 mL |
| 4 | portions of walleye (fillets *or* steaks) 1/3 lb (150 g) | 4 |

## Method

1. In a saucepan, heat the oil and brown the vegetables.
2. Add the tomato sauce, salt and pepper, and cook for 4 to 5 minutes. Add the herbs to this *ratatouille* at the last minute.
3. Meanwhile, in a skillet, bring the stock to a boil. Season to taste and add the oregano.
4. Place the fish in the stock and cook (poach) for 4 to 5 minutes or according to thickness, without boiling.
5. Serve the walleye on a bed of ratatouille with couscous or rice.

# Basil-Marinated Walleye
# with Creamy Red Pepper Sauce

**4 SERVINGS**

## Ingredients

### Marinade

| | | |
|---|---|---|
| **1/4 cup** | oil | **60 mL** |
| **1** | juice of one lemon | **1** |
| **1/4 cup** | fresh basil, chopped | **60 mL** |
| **1** | garlic clove, minced | **1** |

### Sauce

| | | |
|---|---|---|
| **1 tbsp** | butter | **15 mL** |
| **2** | red peppers, chopped fine | **2** |
| **1** | small onion, chopped fine | **1** |
| **1/3 cup** | white wine | **80 mL** |
| **2 tbsp** | sugar | **30 mL** |
| **1/2 cup** | 35% whipping cream | **125 mL** |
| | fresh basil, chopped, as garnish | |
| | salt and fresh ground pepper, to taste | |
| **4** | walleye fillets, 1/3 lb (150 g) each | **4** |
| | **or** | |
| **2.2 lb** | whole walleye | **1 kg** |

## Method

1. Mix all the marinade ingredients and marinate the fish for 30 minutes to 1 hour maximum, in the refrigerator.

2. Meanwhile, melt the butter in a saucepan and brown the pepper and onion.

3. Deglaze with the white wine and reduce by a third. Add the sugar while reducing.

4. Add the cream and cook until desired consistency (the cream thickens during cooking). Check the seasoning.

5. **Fillets *en papillote*:** Preheat the grill to medium-high and cook in an aluminum foil for 10 to 12 minutes.

   **Whole fish:** Preheat the grill to medium-high and cook for 6 to 7 minutes on each side.

6. Serve the fish on a bed of the sauce, and garnish with the fresh basil.

**Note:**

You can use the marinade to baste the walleye while it is cooking to lend more flavor to this delicious recipe.

# Walleye with Creamy Saffron Sauce

## Ingredients

| | | |
|---|---|---|
| 1 tbsp | butter | 15 mL |
| 1/4 cup | French shallots, chopped | 60 mL |
| 1/2 cup | white wine | 125 mL |
| 1/4 tsp | saffron | 1 mL |
| 1 tbsp | butter | 15 mL |
| 4 portions | walleye fillets, 1/3 lb (150 g) each | 4 portions |
| 1 cup | 35% whipping cream | 250 mL |
| 1 tbsp | fresh chives, chopped | 15 mL |
| | salt and fresh ground pepper, to taste | |

## Method

1. In a saucepan, melt the butter over medium-high heat and sauté the shallots for 5 minutes.
2. Deglaze with the wine and add the saffron. Reduce by half over medium-high heat.
3. Meanwhile, melt the butter in a skillet over medium-high heat and cook the fish fillets, turning only once. Season to taste.
4. Add the cream to the wine reduction and continue cooking until the mixture takes on a rich texture. Season to taste.
5. Add the chives to the sauce.
6. Serve the walleye with the sauce and your favorite side dish.

# Northern Pike

Northern pike have a large mouth containing more than 700 sharp teeth. Consummate predators, they regularly eat frogs, ducks, and small mammals, as well as other fish. The species is prized for its brawling, often spectacular fighting qualities. Northern pike have green and brown shades on the head, with lighter spots marking their body. They usually measure from 28 to 39 inches (70 to 100 centimeters) in length and can weigh from 4.4 to 16.5 pounds (2 to 7.5 kilograms). In little-fished waters the occasional fish gets much larger.

The flesh of the Northern pike is pale and fatty and may have a muddy taste. To remove this disagreeable taste, soak the fish in cold water with a bit of vinegar (1 to 2 tablespoons of vinegar per cup of water) for one to two hours before cooking. Northern pike can be prepared in a multitude of ways, such as braised, poached or sautéed. Whatever your approach, it is advisable to fillet the fish or cut it up to remove the skin and numerous bones. Smaller pike taste better than larger ones, but they are more difficult to fillet.

***Note:*** *Do not wash this fish too vigorously, as its viscous coating makes it tenderer.*

# Pears Stuffed with Northern Pike

## Ingredients

| | | |
|---|---|---|
| 1/3 cup | plain yogurt | 80 mL |
| 1 1/2 tbsp | lime juice | 22 mL |
| 2 tsp | curry paste **or** curry powder | 10 mL |
| 1 1/2 cups | cooked Northern pike, flaked | 375 mL |
| 1/4 cup | red pepper, diced small | 60 mL |
| 2 | green onions, chopped | 2 |
| 1/4 cup | cucumber, diced fine | 60 mL |
| | salt and fresh ground pepper, to taste | |
| | fresh chopped coriander, to taste | |
| 2 | fresh ripe *or* canned pears, washed, halved and core removed | 2 |

## Method

1. In a bowl, mix the yogurt, lime juice and curry paste.
2. Add the fish and vegetables.
3. Season to taste and add the coriander.
4. Spoon the fish mixture into the pear halves.
5. Serve the pike-stuffed pears with a small side of lettuce.

**Note:**

To keep the pear half from rocking on the serving plate, cut a thin slice off the round bottom to stabilize it. It is better to use very ripe pears, or to poach them if they are too firm.

# Fish Sausages

## Ingredients

| | | |
|---|---|---|
| 1 lb | Northern pike meat, uncooked | 450 g |
| 2 | egg whites | 2 |
| 1/4 cup | bread crumbs | 60 mL |
| 1/2 cup | 35% whipping cream | 125 mL |
| 1/2 cup | small shrimp, de-veined and chopped | 125 mL |
| 1/2 cup | scallops, coarsely chopped | 125 mL |
| 2 tbsp | oil | 30 mL |
| 1 | leek white, sliced fine | 1 |
| 2 | carrots, finely-chopped | 2 |
| 1/2 cup | red pepper, finely-chopped | 125 mL |
| 2 | garlic cloves, chopped | 2 |
| 1 tbsp | lemon zest | 15 mL |
| 1 tbsp | fresh tarragon, chopped | 15 mL |
| | salt and fresh ground pepper, to taste | |

### Vinaigrette

| | | |
|---|---|---|
| 3/4 cup | olive oil | 180 mL |
| 1 tbsp | sesame seed oil | 15 mL |
| 2 tbsp | fresh-squeezed lemon juice | 30 mL |
| 2 tbsp | tamari (soybean) sauce | 30 mL |
| 1 | garlic clove, minced | 1 |
| 1 tsp | fresh ginger, chopped | 5 mL |
| 1 tsp | fresh tarragon, chopped | 5 mL |

## Method

1. Using a food processor, mix the pike meat, egg whites and bread crumbs until smooth in texture.

2. Slowly add the cream without over-stirring.

3. Pour into a large bowl. Add the shrimp and scallops, mix well and refrigerate.

4. In a skillet, heat 1 tbsp (15 mL) of oil and sauté the vegetables for 5 to 8 minutes. Cool and add to the refrigerated fish mixture. Add the zests and the tarragon. Return to the refrigerator.

5. Place refrigerated fish mixture in a pastry bag. Attach a smooth pastry tube and pipe the mixture out in sausage shapes onto a surface covered with plastic wrap. Wrap each sausage in plastic wrap and twist to seal the ends. Refrigerate for 30 minutes again to firm.

6. Bring 8 cups (2 liters) of water to the boil and carefully drop in the sausages. Boil in the plastic wrap for 8 to 10 minutes. Rinse to cool.

7. Just before serving, heat the remaining oil, remove the plastic wraps and brown the sausages.

8. Slice the sausages into medallions and serve on a bed of lettuce or as delicate appetizers, garnished with lime and a tamari sauce vinaigrette.

### Vinaigrette

1. Thoroughly mix all ingredients together and serve with the fish sausages.

### Brunoise

*A mixture of finely chopped or shredded vegetables cooked slowly in butter.*

# *Index*